Violin
by Craig Duncan

CD CONTENTS

1 Lesson 1 - Open Strings	20 Lesson 9	39 Gavotte in C
2 Lesson 2	21 Riguadon	40 "Marche" from *The Algerian Suite*
3 Twinkle, Twinkle Little Star	22 Lesson 10 - Lavender's Blue	41 Lesson 20
4 Lesson 3	23 Allegretto	42 "Bouree" from the *Water Music*
5 Mary Had a Little Lamb	24 Lesson 11 - Gavotte	43 Etude
6 Jingle Bells	25 Simple Gifts	44 Lesson 21 - "Gavotte" from *Sonata #2, Opus 5*
7 Lesson 4 - Russian Dance Tune	26 Lesson 12 - Fanfare Minuet	45 Minuet
8 Lightly Row	27 King Williams March	46 Lesson 22
9 Camptown Races	28 Lesson 13	47 German Dance
10 Lesson 5	29 London Symphony	48 Lesson 23 - German Dance in A
11 Hungarian Folk Song #1	30 Lesson 14 - Jamaica	49 Andante Grazioso
12 The Old Gray Goose	31 Lesson 15 - British Grenadiers	50 Lesson 24 - Ride, Ride
13 Lesson 6 - Ode to Joy	32 Symphony Theme	51 Bonaparte's Retreat
14 Scherzando	33 Lesson 16 - Minuet	52 Lesson 25 - Soldier's March
15 Lesson 7 - Gavotte	34 The Harmonious Blacksmith	53 "Theme" from the *Fourth Symphony*
16 Country Gardens	35 Lesson 17	54 Lesson 26 - Glockenspiel
17 Can-Can	36 Trumpet Minuet	55 Lesson 27 - Surprise Symphony
18 Lesson 8 - Dixie	37 Lesson 18 - French March	56 Gavotte in D
19 "Largo" from *The New World Symphony*	38 Lesson 19	57 Lesson 28 - Sonatina

It doesn't get any easier.....

1 2 3 4 5 6 7 8 9 0

© 2002 BY MEL BAY PUBLICATIONS, INC., PACIFIC, MO 63069.
ALL RIGHTS RESERVED. INTERNATIONAL COPYRIGHT SECURED. B.M.I. MADE AND PRINTED IN U.S.A.
No part of this publication may be reproduced in whole or in part, or stored in a retrieval system, or transmitted in any form or by any means, electronic, mechanical, photocopy, recording, or otherwise, without written permission of the publisher.

Visit us on the Web at www.melbay.com — E-mail us at email@melbay.com

Introduction

This text presents beginning violin technique and basic music reading fundamentals. There is an emphasis on using melodies and classical pieces to instruct each new concept. The 28 lessons include basic technique and reading skills, scales in the keys of A, D, G and C and bowing techniques such as dynamic contrast, slurs, accents, and staccato bowing. There are 47 melodies presented including works by Bach, Beethoven, Brahms, Handel, Mozart and other classical composers.

A CD recording of the book is available. It has all of the exercises and pieces recorded with solo violin and piano accompaniment. It is useful as a teaching and practice tool as well as a performance accompaniment track.

Contents

Title	Composer	Lesson	page
Andante Grazioso	Wolfgang A. Mozart	Lesson 23	27
Allegretto	Ludwig van Beethoven	Lesson 10	14
Bonaparte's Retreat	Theme from Rodeo	Lesson 24	28
Bourée from The Water Music	Georg Frederic Handel	Lesson 20	24
British Grenadiers		Lesson 15	19
Can Can	Jacques Offenbach	Lesson 7	11
Camptown Races		Lesson 4	8
Country Gardens		Lesson 7	11
Dixie		Lesson 8	12
Etude	Nikolai Paganini	Lesson 20	24
Fanfare Minuet		Lesson 12	16
French March		Lesson 18	22
Gavotte		Lesson 7	11
Gavotte		Lesson 11	15
Gavotte from Sonata No. 2, Opus 5	Georg Frederic Handel	Lesson 21	25
Gavotte in C		Lesson 19	23
Gavotte in D	Arcangelo Corelli	Lesson 27	31
German Dance	Ludwig van Beethoven	Lesson 22	26
German Dance in A	Ludwig van Beethoven	Lesson 23	27
Glockenspiel	Wolfgang A. Mozart	Lesson 26	30
The Harmonious Blacksmith	Georg Frederic Handel	Lesson 16	20
Hungarian Folk Song Number 1	Bela Bartok	Lesson 5	9
Jamaica	English Dance Tune	Lesson 14	18
King William's March	Jeremiah Clarke	Lesson 12	16
Largo from The New World Symphony	Anton Dvorak	Lesson 8	12
Lavender's Blue		Lesson 10	14
Lightly Row		Lesson 4	8
London Symphony	Joseph Haydn	Lesson 13	17
Marche from the Algerian Suite	Camille Saint-Saens	Lesson 19	23
Mary Had a Little Lamb		Lesson 3	7
Menuet	J. S. Bach	Lesson 21	25
Minuet	Georg Philipp Telemann	Lesson 16	20
Jingle Bells		Lesson 3	7
Ode to Joy	Ludwig van Beethoven	Lesson 6	10
The Old Gray Goose		Lesson 5	9
Ride, Ride	Dmitri Kabalevsky	Lesson 24	28
Rigaudon	Henry Purcell	Lesson 9	13
Russian Dance Tune		Lesson 4	8
Scherzando	Bela Bartok	Lesson 6	10
Simple Gifts	Shaker Melody	Lesson 11	15
Soldier's March	Robert Schumann	Lesson 25	29
Sonatina	Ludwig van Beethoven	Lesson 28	32
Surprise Symphony	Joseph Haydn	Lesson 27	31
Symphony Theme	Johannes Brahms	Lesson 15	19
Theme from the Fourth Symphony	Franz Schubert	Lesson 25	29
Trumpet Minuet		Lesson 17	21
Twinkle, Twinkle Little Star		Lesson 2	6

Lesson 1
Holding the Violin

Stand in an erect position with the feet shoulder width apart. Place the violin on the left shoulder, pointing outward to the side. Turn the head to the left and lower the left jaw and chin over the chin rest. The instrument should be supported entirely by the chin and shoulder, so that the left hand is free to note the instrument.

Practice holding the violin parallel to the floor using only the chin and shoulder for support. Place your left hand on your right shoulder and practice holding the violin with "no hands" for 30 seconds, then for a minute and then for two minutes. Do this several times daily until you are comfortable holding the violin with no support from your hands. The neck and shoulder muscles should be as relaxed as possible, using only enough tension to keep the violin from falling.

Many violinists find that a cloth or shoulder rest is helpful in supporting the instrument. There are many styles available. Experiment to determine what is best for you.

The index finger should touch the side of the violin neck at the knuckle adjoining the palm. The thumb should touch the opposite side of the neck above the thumb knuckle which is held in a straight position so that the end of the thumb is pointing upward. This placement will create an opening under the violin neck between the thumb, index finger and palm. The wrist is held with the palm away from the neck so that an imaginary line could be drawn from the elbow to the fingers. The left arm and elbow are held under the violin. The fingertips are to be placed on the strings with the knuckles bent.

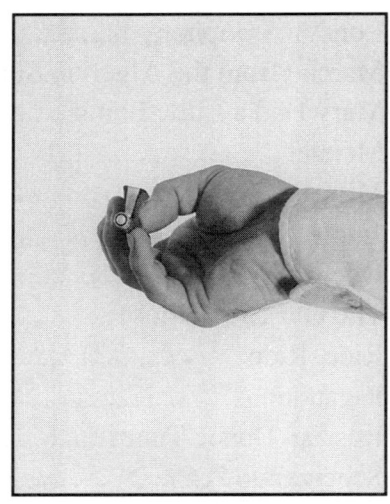

The first finger should touch the bow between the first and second joints. The middle and ring fingers should wrap around the bow comfortably, and the tip of the little finger should rest on the top edge of the bow. The fingers should be curved and spread apart. The end or tip of the thumb should be placed on the bow, forming a circle with the middle finger. The thumb knuckle is bent outward to eliminate tension in the right hand. The grip should be as relaxed as possible, using only enough tension to cradle the bow.

Practice finding the proper bow grip, releasing it, and finding it again at least twenty times before attempting to bow the violin. This is a good warmup exercise to use daily until the bow grip feels comfortable.

Photos by Charmaine Lanham

Playing the Open Strings

The names of the open strings from highest to lowest in pitch are E, A, D and G. They are notated on the following spaces of the treble clef.

Place the bow on the E string midway between the bridge and the fingerboard. Pull the bow across the string in a downward motion toward the floor. This is called "down bow". The opposite direction is called "up bow". Practice going down and up bow several times on each string using short bow strokes. Try to keep the bow moving in a straight direction. It should stay at a ninety degree angle to the string. The right wrist should bend as the bow moves across the string. The right shoulder should be relaxed and the right elbow should stay level with the bow as you move from string to string.

Quarter Notes and Half Notes

The quarter note gets one beat and the half note gets two beats. The whole note gets four beats. The bow direction (down or up) is marked with the following symbols.

Practice these exercises, concentrating on straight bow strokes and clear tone.

Track #2

Lesson 2

The notes in first position on the A string are open A, first finger B, second finger C# and third finger D. The notes on the E string are open E, first finger F#, second finger G# and third finger A. The notes on these two strings combine to make an A scale. Memorize the names of the notes and where they are found on the staff.

Track #3

Twinkle, Twinkle Little Star

Lesson 3

Track #4

The flats or sharps used in the key of a piece of music are shown at the beginning of the staff. This is called a key signature. In the key of A, there are three sharps - F#, C# and G#.

Track #5

Mary Had a Little Lamb

Track #6

Jingle Bells

Track #7

Lesson 4

At the end of *Russian Dance Tune* and *Lightly Row* there are two dots just before the final barline. This is called a **repeat sign** and indicates that the music is to be played again.

When a dot is added after a note, the length of the note is increased by half. Thus a two beat half note followed by a dot becomes a three beat dotted half note. Likewise, a one beat quarter note becomes a one and a half beat dotted quarter note.

Lesson 5

Track #10

The eighth note is equal to one half of a quarter note, so it usually gets one half of a beat. Eighth notes are counted by saying "1 and 2 and 3 and 4 and." When an eighth note follows a dotted quarter it comes on the "and" of the beat.

Track #11

Hungarian Folk Song Number 1

Bela Bartok

Track #12

The Old Gray Goose

Lesson 6

Track #13

The notes in first position on the D string are open D, first finger E, second finger F# and third finger G. Memorize the names of the notes and where they are found on the staff.

Ode to Joy (Ninth Symphony Theme)

Ludwig van Beethoven

Rests

A rest is a symbol which means to be silent. There is a rest equal to the value of each kind of note.

Eighth rest ♫ = one half beat   Quarter rest 𝄽 = one beat   Half rest ▬ = two beats   Whole rest ▬ = four beats

Scherzando

Bela Bartok

10

Lesson 7
D Scale

When two sharps, F# and C#, are found at the beginning of the staff, the music is in the key of D. A D scale can be played using the notes in first position on the D and A strings. Memorize the names of the notes and where they are played on your instrument.

Gavotte

Country Gardens

Can, Can
Jacques Offenbach

Track #18

Lesson 8
Dynamics

The violin can be played louder or softer by changing three things:
1. The amount of bow pressure on the string; more pressure is louder, less pressure is softer.
2. The speed of the bow; faster bow is louder, slower bow is softer.
3. Closeness of the bow to the bridge; closer is louder, away from the bridge is softer.

The symbols for how loud or soft music is played are called **dynamic** markings.

ff double forte — very loud   *f* forte — loud   *mf* mezzo forte — medium loud   *mp* mezzo piano — medium soft   *p* piano — soft   *pp* double piano — very soft

Dixie

Largo from The New World Symphony
Anton Dvorak

Lesson 9

The notes in the key of D on the E string are open E, first finger F#, low second finger G and third finger A. The low second finger is placed on the string very close to the first finger creating a half step interval between the two fingers. The third finger stays in its same postion, leaving a whole step between second and third finger.

Rigaudon

Henry Purcell

Lesson 10

At the beginning of the first staff just after the key signature is a symbol called the **time signature**. Everything found in the book so far has been in "common" time which is the same as 4/4. The tunes in this lesson are in 3/4. The top number in the time signature gives the number of beats per measure and the bottom number tells what kind of note is equal to one beat. In "common" time, marked with a C, and in 4/4 time there are four beats per measure and the quarter note is equal to one beat. In 3/4 time there are three beats per measure and the quarter note is equal to one beat.

Lavender's Blue

Allegretto

Ludwig van Beethoven

Lesson 11

A **slur** is a marking that connects two or more notes. All notes connected by a slur are played without changing the direction of the bow. A slur that connects two notes on the same pitch is called a **tie**.

Gavotte

Simple Gifts

Shaker Melody

Lesson 12
Accents

Accents are found on notes that are to be emphasized or played stronger than notes around them. This is done by applying more bow pressure at the beginning of the note. Once the note begins the pressure is lightened to the normal amount.

Fanfare Minuet

King William's March
Jeremiah Clarke

Track #28

Lesson 13
Key of G

The key of G has only one sharp, F#. The second finger is placed low on the E string to play G natural and low on the A string to play C natural. The first finger pattern is used on th G string to play G, A, B and C. Memorize the names of the notes in the key of G and where they are on the instrument.

Track #29

London Symphony
Joseph Haydn

Track #30

Lesson 14
Crescendo and Decrescendo

Crescendo means to play gradually louder and decrescendo means to play gradually softer. Sometimes the words or an abreviation (cresc and decresc) are used in the music. Other times the symbol < indicates crescendo, getting louder, and the symbol > indicates decrescendo, getting softer.

Jamaica

English Dance Tune

Lesson 15
The Upbeat

Music often begins with less than the full number of beats in the first measure. These notes are called pickups. The first beat of a full measure is called the downbeat and the last beat of a measure is called the upbeat. Upbeats are usually played up bow.

British Grenadiers

Symphony Theme
Johannes Brahms

Lesson 16
Accidentals

Accidentals are sharps, flats or natural signs that are used when the note in the music is not in the key signature. They change the notes for only one measure at a time. In the following measure the notes in the key signature are used unless there is another accidental marking.

Minuet
Georg Philipp Telemann

The Harmonious Blacksmith
Georg Frederic Handel

Lesson 17
Key of C

The key of C has no sharps or flats. The first finger pattern is used on the G string. The D string and A string have low second fingers. The first finger on the E string is also played low. This new finger pattern places the first finger an half step from the open string with a whole step between first and second and second and third fingers. Memorize the names of these notes and where they are played on the violin.

Trumpet Minuet

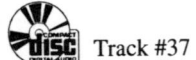 Track #37

Lesson 18

There are two lines to this tune. The top line is the melody or first violin part and the bottom line is the harmony or second violin part. Learn to play each part, then play a duet by putting the parts together with another musician.

The word **ritard** found at the end of the piece means to slow down.

French March

Lesson 19

Track #38

Sometimes it is necessary to play two notes with the same bow direction but make them sound as if the bow direction changed. This is done by stopping the bow and then starting again, continuing the same direction. Try to make the notes sound as if each were a seperate bow stroke.

Gavotte in C

Track #39

Marche from the Algerian Suite

Camille Saint-Saens

Track #40

Lesson 20

Track #41

The fourth finger of the left hand is very important in playing the violin. In first position, fourth finger on the A string should sound the same pitch as open E, fourth finger on the D the same as open A, and fourth finger on the G the same as open D. Fourth finger on the E string is B.

Bourrée from The Water Music
Georg Frederic Handel

Track #42

Etude
Nikolai Paganini

Track #43

Lesson 21

Track #44

There is often a choice of playing either the open string or the fourth finger. A good rule to follow is to use the fingering that makes the bowing smoother. For example, the first measure of this piece is played on the A string without a string crossing when the fourth finger is used to play the E.

Gavotte from Sonata No. 2, Opus 5
Georg Frederic Handel

Menuet
J. S. Bach

Track #45

Lesson 22
Key of A

The key of A has three sharps, F#, C# and G#. A two octave scale can be played beginning with first finger A on the G string. The third finger on the G string is played a whole step higher than the second finger to note C#. The third finger on the D string is also played higher to note G#.

German Dance
Ludwig van Beethoven

Lesson 23
German Dance in A

Track #48

Ludwig van Beethoven

Andante Grazioso

Track #49

Wolfgang Amadeus Mozart

Lesson 24

Sixteenth notes have two flags and are half as long as eighth notes. In 4/4, 3/4 and 2/4 time there are four sixteenth notes in each beat.

Ride, Ride

Dmitri Kabalevsky

Bonaparte's Retreat
Theme used by Aaron Copland for Rodeo

Lesson 25

Track #52

The dotted eighth gets three fourths of a beat. It is equal to the length of three sixteenth notes. Make certain to make it last three times longer than the sixteenth note in these melodies.

Soldier's March
Robert Schumann

Theme from the Fourth Symphony
Track #53

Franz Schubert

Track #54

Lesson 26

Staccato markings are dots found over or under the note head. They indicate that the note is to be played with a shorter bow stroke, stopping the bow before the full value of the note sounds. This leaves space between the notes giving them a "short" sound.

Glockenspiel

Wolfgang A. Mozart

30

Lesson 27

Track #55

The following tunes have staccato notes and full length notes. Be certain to make a difference in the style by leaving space between the staccato notes while the bow is stopped and playing full bow strokes on the notes that are not staccato.

Surprise Symphony
Joseph Haydn

Gavotte in D
Arcangelo Corelli

Track #56

Track #57

Lesson 28

Grace notes are small notes written just before a regular size note. They do not last the normal length, but are played quickly. In some pieces they are played on the beat and in other pieces they are played before the beat.

Sonatina

Ludwig van Beethoven